SO-AZT-786

RESCUE

SALLY ALLEN MCNALL

The Backwaters Press

Also by Sally Allen McNall

How To Behave at the Zoo and Other Lessons, State Street Press, 1997

Photo of the poet © Alain Tomatis, 2000.

Cover photograph © Scott McNall, 2000.

All poems Copyright © Sally Allen McNall, 2000, if not otherwise noted.

Backwaters Press Logo designed by L. L. Mannlein, Copyright © 1997,
The Backwaters Press

All rights reserved. No part of this book may be reproduced in any form, except
for the inclusion of brief quotations in a review, without permission in writing
from the author or the publisher.

First Printing, 300 copies, March 2000.

Published by: The Backwaters Press
                        Greg Kosmicki, Editor/Publisher
                        3502 North 52nd Street
                        Omaha, Nebraska 68104-3506
                        (402) 451-4052
                        GKosm62735@AOL.com

ISBN : 0-9677149-0-7

LIBRARY OF CONGRESS CATALOG CARD NUMBER: 00-131733

Printed in the United States by
Morris Publishing • 3212 East Highway 30 • Kearney, NE 68847
1-800-450-7888

Acknowledgements

"Down tree," *Portland Review Literary Journal* (Winter, 1998): 96.

"A Wedding in Antwerp," *Seattle Review* (Spring 1998): 38-39.

"Jewel," *Crab Creek Review* (Summer/Autumn,1999): 60.

"Heart Failure," *13th Moon* (Vol. XV, nos. 1 and 2): 179-181.

"Amnion," *Cottonwood Review* (Fall 1998): 16-17.

"Builder," "El Malpais" (as "Occasional Poem"), "Sweet Basil," *Kansas Quarterly*, (Summer 1988):145-148.

"Premonition," Arctos Press Anthology, *GRRRRR* (1999).

"A Teaching" (as "A Lesson"), *The MacGuffin* (Spring, 1999):46.

"Madeline in a Prospect of Flowers," *This Little Bit of Earth*, Valley Oaks Press, 1997.

"Solstice," *Primavera* (Vol 22, 1999): 61-62.

"Water garden," *Permafrost* (Fall, 1997): 42-44.

"Stars falling," "Sun Setting," *The MacGuffin* (Spring, 1998): 15-20.

"Seeing it," *Panhandler* (Winter 1990), 29-30.

"Three Poems," *Cincinnati Poetry Review* (Spring/Summer 1995): 9-12.

"History Lesson," *Cincinnati Poetry Review* (forthcoming).

"Studio," *The MacGuffin* (Fall, 1999): 152.

The poems "Tremor," "Private life" (as "Daily life"), "Seeing it," "Stars falling," and "Sun setting" are included in the chapbook *How to Behave at the Zoo and Other Lessons*, State Street Press, 1997.

Many thanks to these supporters of The Backwaters Press without whose generous contributions and subscriptions the publication of this book would not have been possible.

ANGELS

Steve and Kathy Kloch
Greg and Barb Kuzma
Don and Marjorie Saiser
Rich and Eileen Zochol

BENEFACTORS

Barbara Schmitz

PATRONS

Guy and Jennie Duncan
Cheryl Kessell
Maureen Toberer
Frederick Zydek

SPONSORS

Paul and Mildred Kosmicki
Gary Leisman and Wendy Adams
Jeff and Patty Knag
Matt Mason
Pat Murray and Jeanne Schuler
Anne Potter
Carol Schmid
Alan and Kim Stoler
Don Taylor

FRIENDS

J. V. Brummels
Twyla Hansen
Tim O'Connor
Jim and Mary Pipher
Richard White

SALLY ALLEN MCNALL

RESCUE

Winner of the 1999 Backwaters Prize

Rescue

Shell hunt

- 1 Ghosts
- 2 Down tree
- 3 Stone
- 4 A Wedding in Antwerp
- 5 Cedilla
- 6 Jewel
- 7 Blackberries
- 8 Coda
- 9 Heart Failure
- 12 Shell hunt

Amnion

- 15 Amnion
- 16 Sweet Basil
- 17 Design
- 18 Danger
- 19 Flight
- 20 Petitionary prayer
- 21 Fear of strangers
- 22 Slowly
- 23 Premonition
- 24 Bare Ground
- 25 What is to be done

Studio

- 29 El Malpais
- 30 Builder
- 31 A Teaching
- 32 Failure to profit from solitude
- 33 Tremor
- 34 Madeline in a Prospect of Flowers
- 35 Next time
- 36 Studio
- 37 Solstice
- 38 Gifts
- 40 Water Garden

Natural boundaries

- 45 Host
- 46 Stars falling
- 48 Sun setting
- 50 Epeirogeny
- 52 The Limits of Language
- 54 Seeing It
- 56 Three Poems
- 59 History Lesson
- 60 Today
- 61 Power
- 62 The Quiet of Volcanoes
- 63 Manzanita
- 64 Natural boundaries
- 67 Rescue

To Miles, Amy, and their children

Shell hunt

Ghosts

Just below the surface of sleep
I suddenly miss your black Olds Cutlass.
Thirteen years since you sold
that sweet baby and here it is
heavy in my heart— I'm wide awake,
wanting it back, top down, you and me in the hot wind.

Really, what hope is there? What can't
we grieve senselessly over?
Last night I spoke with other women
about refugees, how displaced hearts
may trip over great losses but minds go on,
work the story right, somehow.

Among them, I realized as I talked,
was a girl whose boy died last fall
in a plane crash— a small plane he piloted.
There's no beginning or end to it, is there?
Our broken hearts can't move along with our minds,
our acquired fluencies and comforting habits.

How hopelessly stubborn we must be
if an absurd object a happy person
hasn't thought about in years
can return a sleek ghost, gorging
on gas and adrenaline,
grinning that no heart is safe.

Down tree

—for my father

Seventy years ago, you could take
the mountain trail, over a suspension
bridge, all the way to the shore.
First growth, all up and down
the coast. You were an Eagle Scout,
and often one of a net of boys and men
seining for the lost in that wildness.
Here, where the forest's been protected,
is how it was: growth so thick
you had to hack your way through, calling
from time to time to the others deep
to your left and right in the cold shade,
under hemlock, alder, cedar, spruce,
through salal, bracken and fern, over down
trees and the small complexity of lives
their dying sustains. You went over streams,
under trees dead but still standing, thick
around as the reach of six boys, draped
with moss, circled with shell-shaped fungus.

Today, before we head back, you stop,
square in the middle of the new broad, smooth trail.
You say, "No more," and as usual
I have to guess at your meaning. We start, more slowly now,
back to the highway that cut the old trail
off from the sea. When we pass the great
down tree again we both graze
its gray whorls with the flat of our hands.

Stone

When his mother was a girl in the orphanage she couldn't eat in the big hall.
She was hungry all the rest of the time. She missed the Minnesota woods,
picking berries, trapping rabbits, before her mother ran away. She learned the
chant for scrubbing stone floors: *up down to the right down up down to the left.*

* * *

He goes back and forth between kitchen and garden in the Sierra Nevada,
getting a glass of water, a sandwich, more water. Today he lays a stretch of brick
walk, mends deer fence, feeds roses. There's nothing he'd rather do. Our
daughter comes over in the afternoon to help with the garden. Around four
o' clock she goes inside and begins to put together one of the big pasta dinners
he loves. He loves the kitchen in this mess, opens wine, pour us each a glass.

* * *

His mother, old, and alone again today, cleans and cleans the house. Nothing is
out of place. In her garden, everything's cut back, picked, raked. She eats her
meals standing.

* * *

Our granddaughter runs away from the table again. She's too busy to eat, she has
to clean up all our spills, dragging the blue kitchen stool over to get one paper
towel, then another. Over, and back again. She's brought rocks in from the
yard, and while the rest of us eat, she folds each in its own fresh towel on the
floor, singing "poor stone, dear stone, poor stone, dear stone."

A Wedding in Antwerp

The life of the table, said the art historian,
is the life of all human times and places,
a cup, knife, apple ready to any hand.
To paint these humble things the artist need only
observe, transcribe the daily domestic round,
the obverse of sublime. Here, nothing happens.

See how I stand, said the tall rosemary sprig,
in the tarte's center, hung with gold
ornament. *Over here, and over here*, said pastries
like sugared lace. *We are most uncommon.*
Three shells breathed, *we are rare*, and a paper twist
of spice said, *from far away.* The porcelain cup,
gilt mounted, the pitcher to match, the slender flute
of Venetian glass, the ripe fruits of the south
said, *Notice: we're perfect. You'd hesitate,*
were we real, to disturb our fine composure.

The art historian said, all is vanity.
You are meant to see how any human life
is only a moment, and all these glittering things
are finally useless, really don't matter at all.

I looked for the painter's name. Clara Peeters.
We don't know her dates, no document survives
of her life but her work. And does that matter?

The art historian said, this might be a bridal
banquet. Ah— then something has happened.

I mean fidelity, says the rosemary.
The knife says *fides*, the red anemones
crossed beneath the knife, the sugar dainties,
are gifts for such an occasion. Must we explain
the three oysters? Oh, Clara, Clara,
this time, I think, you said to yourself, *Nothing's*
too good. Only a moment? Maybe, but I
will keep faith with the life of the body,
that eats and drinks and prolongs its meticulous loves.
My hands are filled with their treasure.

Cedilla

—for Ginger

When you call me today
we're both home, haven't gone out.

"It's a *cedilla*," you announce in triumph, and I
remember at once how last week at dinner we knew
it wasn't a *tilde* we meant, but didn't feel up
to getting out the dictionaries.

"I thought I'd better call while I could
remember."

In good camouflage a person disappears
into leaves, tree bark, water, forest floor,
snow. Disappears. In the Cabela catalogue
there are eight regional variations of hunter's camo.
We hide out all day in bathrobes,
staring into our dark waters or snowfields,
waiting patiently for movement, waiting patiently
to remember what it was like.

Your voice is roughened again by some new infection.
"Two and a half days at work," you laugh,
"and I'm sick again." We've listed together
what we might do to protect
our bodies' immunity. We don't know as much
as the trout in their rainbows know
of what leaches slowly into their rivers.

"Take care of yourself," I say, take care
of the *cedilla*, the *umlaut*. Don't disappear.
Remember how when you were three or even four
at the height of summer you used to strip naked
and run outside before they could catch you?
Remember? "Take care of the *accent aigu*."
Protect your immunity.

Jewel

Someone was explaining at length the process
by which the outer skin of the bamboo
is made into the paper which bonds best with gold leaf.
This paper flutters— like the flames of candles
or like doves brought for sacrifice— on Buddhas.

Someone else was going to see the Romanov Treasure.

And of course there was talk, as always that spring,
of the comet. I myself claimed the best sighting,
for I live in arid hills, saw it with the crescent moon,
bracketed by tall pines. Darkness behind everything.

Yet what beside the darkness doesn't reflect the light?
Though some love strips you, some may be worn
like glass bangles or chainmail, glinting at the least movement.
The stripped soul blazes. But I mean you to wear
this love in the hollow of your throat.

Blackberries

The first autumn rain
loosens the last dark sweetness
from the wild unpicked blackberries.
You stop, close your eyes as if against a wind,
against all you waited
through your long youth
to find.

Coda
—for Diane

Your heartbroken old dog, blind, weeps as he turns around
lost under the table. We pretend it's not happening.

On the radio, Dvorak's Concerto in B minor.
On cello, Jacqueline Du Pre, who died at forty-two of multiple sclerosis.
Impossible not to read this back into the music!
The first movement, passion so strong it is pain— it takes
the whole orchestra to calm that young cellist down,
the whole concerto to win her acceptance.

Or else this is nonsense,
the cellist exquisitely happy, that day in Chicago.

And the dog's sounds may mean only that his lungs and throat
won't let him make a stronger sound.
His bumbling around at our feet, for all I know,
may revisit the way he carried on as a pup.

As our talk over the last wine revisits the vast silliness
of our early years. As we laugh ourselves into tears.

HEART FAILURE

I. *1991: Autobiographies*

All morning I've been reading the novel again,
aching over it, alone in the old house,
trying to forgive Cather her terror of time.
Only "twenty good years" and the woman writing
already forty-two. How some hearts deny
their strength, pile years up like a circle of stones,
a firepit to burn in. Cather finally got out,
I think, sigh, and make another lengthy note
for a lecture about The Modern Artist.

But I want to go back again with what I know
now, to one of my childhood summers at the lake
when my great aunt Carolyn seemed strong and free.

I want to go back to another summer
when Carolyn's heart was so thickly swollen
her whole body was jarred by each beat.
"You can't be a writer now," said the letter
from the hospital. Then, in a phone call, "Please forgive
me that awful letter. Of course I don't mean it."

So now I close the book, and examine
the pain around my strong heart. I need that voice
again, needing, taking, giving— want to hear it:

II. *1976: House*

Even after Marjorie's mind began to fail
she said she would stay in this house, she would give
nothing away— stubborn as always, the sister
they called the good one. Amy was beautiful. And I,
the responsible one. The one who year after year
paid the bills, hired help and repairmen, made plans.
Sold the lake cottage, saving only the books.

Here, the Chinese rugs have faded, the furniture
is scratched and dull. Tina can't stay long enough
to get things clean— to Marjorie she's a stranger.
But we can still be quite content! Last night we watched
a special on TV about wild ducks. We had
our hot milk in good cups. Our fights don't always end
in tears. Marjorie reads me her old letters
over and over, too pleased to throw them away.
The letters I keep are Sally's. She's so far from here.
I read them over in the long nights and write back.
I write about my old dream of living alone,
Sarton's *Journal of a Solitude*. Could I do
that? Could she? We don't know. We recount
our daily disasters and noble deeds as if
we were one age. "A flame the wind cannot blow out—"
That's Millay, I copied it to send. "Over dark
water the sun went down, a bursting heart." That's mine,
I won't send it. I'm often short of breath now—
on the stairs, and for fear I can't get it all done
in time. Lists, appointments with doctors and lawyers,
our friends' visits. Women only get one chance to escape
such duties, though I don't know when mine went past.
I wonder what Sally knows and doesn't tell me:

III. *1972: Biographies*

The sun's an enemy in this desert country,
I hate it. Even at midnight the air's heavy,
and there's not much that's uplifting about our lives.
Every hour a chore— we drive through a white heat
to teach, to study, to take to school whatever
the kids forgot at home, then to get groceries home.
Trips, papers, parties, lectures, picnics, museums.
Like the machine on the ocean floor in the story,
grinding out salt salt salt. We run, we swim, for miles.
But I dream of a green lake shore, wake up to write
to Carolyn at dawn— who worries, and warns me
I can't have everything. I've nothing! Not true,
but neither are my wonderful letters to her.
She loves me in the same fantastical way I love
John Keats. But I'm not dead, not early dead, not yet.

I sit outside to write, before the sun can top
the walls. In winter months, sometimes, a cardinal comes,
bounces and flames on the olive tree. I can
tell her that. She wants me to be happy, and so
for her I am. Will be. I'm strong enough for that,
I think she is, but I don't know how to ask.
If I can imagine John Keats in Italy,
I ought to know what one day of her life is like:

IV. *1968: Lake*

The second week of June, my job to check the cottage— stove
and plumbing, blankets, see what needs to be fixed.
See the grass is mowed, down to the pebbled shore.
New shingles here and there. Check the cupboards for food
they'll need, for signs of mice. The last visitors
in August will be Sally, her husband, the children.
In the largest bedroom, all the books I've given
her to read, summer after summer— *Little Women*,
later, *Song of the Lark*, this year, *To the Lighthouse*.

It can't be kept up another year, with so few
caring to come back to visit now. In fall,
I will close it for the last time. It takes my breath
away— no more nephews and nieces, all the children
in wet swim suits, hide and seek, new packs of cards,
reading *The Tempest* aloud, trooping out all together
to watch sunset kindle the lake. Just inside
the screen porch, I stop, the door half open, key in hand.
I hope I've forgotten something, stand there, wait.

Shell hunt

—for Dan

You know how it
takes hold of you,
the whole day sometimes.

And the false peace
of sun, sea sound, air

so you don't notice
that you can't stop.

One more. The right
one more.

I thought of you
through thousands of miles.

A pink one. A speckled one.
See how these
fit together. Broken. Whole.

New Zealand 1983-California 1997

12

Amnion

Amnion

I paid no mind for a week to steady pains
before this woman I lean to bathe was born.

Her face distends, eyes swim, with fever.
I lave her tender skin as if she were again my newborn,
copper smell of water, soap, sweat in her hair.

Go on, go on cupping water down the bend
of her back, over the shape of her shoulders,
breasts, one still heavy with milk, slack belly,

while the tired baby who had her bath first
tugs at my wet sleeve, sings her distress
we aren't all still in the press and pour of water.

I bend forward now, back aching.
Pain gentles us all forward in one direction.
There are no ideas about this, only the stunned grace

of how we hoist each other to our feet,
how the baby stretches still for the torn, tilting water.

Sweet Basil

—for Marianne

In the wet dark of the autumn
moment, the mounds of basil
burn, green fire. Fragile towers
tip each thick stem with
small pale flowers; it's plain
the plant is on its way to seed.
It is the last of the crop. Pesto's
in every pot— which is why
the man with the basil is giving it
away. And the car, sluiced by October
morning rain, smells like summer
as we drive back, talking of
timing. You think the worst may be
just what one needs. Just then.
Conception, you tell me, becomes
more difficult as we get older.
Another one of the things
they didn't tell us in time.
I watch your hands fold in your lap.
The slide of the wiper blade is like
a metronome. Frozen in jars,
the pesto will stay green till Christmas.
A gift, I think. Perhaps a gift.

Design

—for Laura

Inside six or twelve little painted matrushkas,
bright kerchiefs and aprons and cheeks,
an embryo or is it Venus? a fetish? featureless,
almost shapeless, saying the impossible: there's more to come.

We go for a walk in the park near the art museum.
Ducks on the pond. Little girls in bonnets with ribbons.
You, in your huge romper patterned like a piesanka,
an egg dark with geometrical designs from the east
thousands and thousands of years old. Nobody knows what they mean.

Danger

1.

Trying to read, and failing
when the hot child shifts in my arms,
I think nothing can contain the seizure of this love
except the miserable job it is.
No one has or wants any chance here
in this small, stunned paradise.

2.

A baby doesn't seem to think about her feet
as she works at the *barre* of the coffee table,
learns to stand, to step sideways. Her attention
is all outside herself. She wins, gives a war cry.

Is that how we know we've lost, by the sounds
we let helplessly loose? No, first pain teaches
our bodies to us, tedious as the first
biology book, with its divided obsessions.

How good to use the body without fear, be called
like evacuees out of our habits, by some final battle,
to let the guerrillas of pleasure and ease surround us—
guns aimed at our doped drudges of hearts, set hopping again.

3.

One newborn demands to be wrapped up.
Another will fall asleep only
on your shoulder. One needs your song
and one must be danced into rest.

So you danced yourself into danger, did you?
Misfortune, pain you almost can't bear?

A small weight will shift in your tight mind.
Shift and sleep. Not often.
Often enough.

Flight

In the airport, at the departure gate, you look over your two small boys to see what will need to be done for them in preparation for the next moment. I'm flying to where one of my children lives. This year I've seen as much as I want to of earth from the sky— mountains I won't climb, fields maybe in South Dakota, maybe Minnesota, lights of cities I don't even bother to identify. How to learn to look closely?

You have moments of surprise at how you love your sons, I know. I'm surprised— on the ground— by the oddest little things.

In the salt desert of India, children wear mirrors in their hats, mirrors, to flash back sun to a parent's eyes if they have wandered too far off.

My eyes a mirror. Your eyes.

Petitionary prayer

Surely you've seen a roomful of babies begin to cry
because one does. We've nothing to teach children

about the unfairness of this life, they know what we
have practiced and practiced to forget, and succeeded.

When we ask a child to reverse the pleasant and important task
of taking all her clothes from her dresser drawers

or to put back the cookies on the supermarket shelf
we talk at length of help, of what is owed others.

Of course our children become confused,
and shut each other up in closets.

Is it our job to teach them that the innocent suffer?
That no one can help herself alone?

That history steadily makes its way
into their lives? It has already. Already
we should kneel with them each morning to cry.

Fear of strangers

Leann's baby has just begun to cry whenever he sees
someone new on his morning stroller ride
through the city neighborhood.

In our animal brain as it grows, a command uncoils: you cannot
love everyone. No one can disobey, though some brains
can revise it a little. We all learn those lessons.
But something else happens that isn't a lesson.
A kid's hormones kick in and for a time
all the signals change again. Our young bodies work to repair
fear's damage. We talk to strangers, we take terrible risks.
Sometimes our older bodies stay humbled by this command.

Leann's baby— if he is lucky— will live through the playground, streets,
high school hallways, triple-locked doors, to love.
List the people you know how to love.
If you had more time— if we added our lifetimes together—

Slowly

—for Denise

In this backyard again, the two women sit
with their coffee, sort through the improbable prairie weather
of their lives, tornadoes, drought, hail the size of eggs, and days
like today— clear sky and bloom, clouds like gathered blossom.

Once they shared a spring soup at this table, asparagus from the garden.
That year, they still believed they could make everything
come out right, if they were willing to stay up all night
talking and crying. The question between them was simple:
Is love true? and the answer *yes*.

Yesterday one of them set purple pansies in the earth
which hasn't time for them in the seed. The other
went with a little boy to the playground. His game was to see
how slowly he could climb the long blue tube slide. She
counted, "1059, 1060," and watched his shadow
move, stop, move inside the bright blue.

She tells her friend about it. Inside their lives
The answer *yes* travels darkly, steadily, becoming true.

Premonition

A hard shiver
on an August afternoon
on the screened porch, book
full of old forests and shipwrecks on my knees.
Two men have set off in a canoe, in white water,
to test their skill. Elsewhere, a young couple
pack their baby into bear country.

Have we had enough hero stories?
Isn't there a *marchen*, somewhere in Grimm,
about giving babies to bears, and
an American story of transformation, children sent to be
bears, stronger and safer than children?

At nightfall, the men explain—
the canoe flipped, rolled in the rapids.
One tells how he came up under it, fought free,
fished gear out onto the river bank,
netted the wallets a plastic bag buoyed up.
They spread money to dry on the dinner table.

In the morning, we hear how the mother grizzly
dropped on all fours and disappeared
up the path, her two cubs after her.

I thought I would be more patient at this age.

Bare Ground

Mother asks how I can think of my grandchildren growing up.
I say I don't think. We know I lie, but we let it go.

I bend over to hold her— skewed shoulder, slowly shattering spine.
We mean well, though there's no grace nor yielding in our embrace.

She won't tell me of the grasslands and water meadows where she played
as a child, refuses to name for me the flowers I will never see.

On hard bare ground the young father built his sweat lodge; to soften
his pain he lay down where the ground was bare.

Do you remember the truth, Mother? The thought that is prayer?

What is to be done

1.

In Beijing in the winter of 'eighty-three
there were billboards everywhere— parents
and one small, tender daughter in a bright silk jacket.
No one on the busy streets wore new clothes
but the children, who went in green and red and gold.

How they have loved them, their only children!
Poured into them every month's shining ration
of oil and expectation!

In China our one daughter showed off for our hosts,
walked behind us, brought us
covered cups of green tea.

I don't know if she will have more than one child.
My small granddaughter brings me tea slowly, seriously.

2.

Will paper money char, curl, smoke out
those Chinese parents in the next life?
How many descendants are required?
Who will visits our graves, bringing flowers?

3.

We watch and worship
these light little creatures in motion, who thrive for now
on our inconsequent love.

Studio

El Malpais

So gradual I think I may have missed
something, but when I turn
back all is changed there, too.

So quiet that I watch
a long time, before I see
what I see.

When I was twelve
I walked with my father
onto a lava flow.
Looking where I put my feet,
I was sure
a cloud had crossed the sun.
I looked up. It blazed as usual.

But my spine knew a storm
was near; I had to hold myself
still.

Today, as I see the leaves
start to release
the light they have stored
all summer,
I don't move. I don't need
to move. I am being taken somewhere.

Builder

Digging, you turn over
rock after rock
the soil's jammed with—
yellow jagged
leftovers of limestone
hills. First, you toss
and pile, anyhow, just
to make way for a garden,
then you imagine: against
the wet bank, sogged
already in long weeds,
a wall. Piece by
piece, a puzzle, since
it's mainly to use it up,
the rock pile. No
mortar mixing and smoothing
at the edge between
vegetables and grass,
only the wedged weight
of the rocks you pick,
turn over and over,
place, replace, pick
like squash, or peppers,
to make something, something
good, gathered, original.

1986

A Teaching

How the old city wants me back!
This bridge is the very shape memory makes in the brain,
heavy bearer of unrelenting traffic.
The tamed waterfall drives my heart down
and down over its combed surface
as it drove the mills for a hundred years.

When the mind is a coffin
wanting to keep all its dead, wanting to bury them all

something says I can break you open, says
look: this is my unforgiving cloud cover,
these are my towers of stained brick and stone,
my winter trees, my bare streets in the hard wind

and you must learn from them
what I always intended to teach you.

If you become empty, so much the better.

Minneapolis, 1965/1995

Failure to profit from solitude

You're out of town, so I go alone to Gounod's Romeo and Juliet.

In the play, the lovers just miss a life together, don't even get a goodbye—
in the French opera, they die singing together, a recap of the aubade:
Believe me, love, in the original English, *it was the nightingale.*

Believe me, love, I think. Love. A variation arrived under domestication,
as Darwin might phrase it, putting the familiar before the strange
natural state, for his domesticated readers.

Arrived for you and me, now entering so naturally
the shadow where these young lovers lie so strangely,
singing supine and stuck, by a dagger, a poison cup.

Darwin imagined not nightingales but elephants unchecked,
imagined nineteen million. I know the number of elephants now in their
natural state. I know it now appears that evolution happens after disasters.

I remember DNA strung like fluorescent green hishi in a magazine photograph.
The intercrossing of individuals patches up defects, says the writer.
A combination stronger than anything a creature can produce alone.

You little glowworms, I think, all you cared for was survival.
But now I am like the poor addled girl in the play
before she quite woke up: *Where is my Romeo?*

Tremor

—for Sandie

I thought you'd never come back from the Midwest
you write, and I want to say I'm not back yet,
you must know that.
We promised at seventeen not to grow up.
I don't know if you've been faithful. It's kept me busy,
getting up each morning with my demands
on landscapes, on decades, on the grand clamor of language and love.

This return West is such work! I'm staggered by my senses—
the smell of eucalyptus, or ocean, the colors of forest, the feel
of the ground's casual tremor.
What were we thinking of then?
Now I have to examine each stone and lichen
as if (but there's no "as if") it were lost and found.

Do you remember the day your little boy disappeared,
how, my little boy in tow, we searched and searched the park,
the neighbor's houses, and found yours at last
in his own bed? Were we very frightened? Because
I don't remember thinking we wouldn't find him. We did
find him. We didn't wake him, but sat down
on the floor , hushed my boy, and wondered
at their sleeping faces, at each other's.

This return is a little like that.

Madeline in a Prospect of Flowers

We have Sunday, all of us, the first Sunday of a whole week off.
We drive an hour up the dirt road to Table Mountain, to see wildflowers
together, and the wild sky all around, the crazy colliding clouds.
Two and a half, you herded us out to the car for the ride
let's go let's go, and sing as we go, of mailboxes, chickens and pickup trucks.
We pass trailers of old couples who've staked out their days on five acres
            of hillside,
the whole Butte County Historical Society Annual Barbecue and plant sale,
and two women by a Buick in their Sunday clothes, having a serious argument.

We walk out on Table Mountain as if onto tundra, mosses, chunks
            of volcanic rock,
flowers like constellations. Whole families spread out picnics and try to get kites
            in the air.
Every grownup on this cold lava flow looks tired and alert for trouble.
We grit our teeth, grin, try not to think about prices or Congress or freeways
or Monday, or what we hate or fear about the jobs we have or don't.
We look up at the sky, down at the flowers, the kids this very minute.

You hunker down to poke *we don't pick* the pink, the blue star, white mallow,
little wild lupine, rock rose, primrose, daisy goldfields *oh flowers oh look look.*
In pinafore and hightops you squat and croon to the yellow stars about you,
get both hands into the soaked black earth. My blossom, you are not a bit
            like a flower.
You declare each day a flower and we believe you, against all evidence.

Next time

After your bath, we'd sit on the floor
where the oil stove breathed into the room
and let it sift your fine little boy hair through my fingers.
And later in another house you bent your head,
the narrow nape of your pale boy's neck
to me and the hairdryer, before I'd let you out into winter.

When did I stop? I've no idea. I've no idea when anything
stopped, was *the last time*, and here I am drying
your child's hair, my fingertips holding, under softness,
the solid shape of mystery. What does this boy know of me?
What will he always know?

Because for me nothing has ever stopped.
"They stopped loving each other." I don't get it,
no matter how often it's explained— emergency rooms,
reptilian indifference, locks, no forwarding address,
crazy children and parents gone to live on the street.

Could I still open my arms to the first boy I promised to love forever,
to men and women I haven't seen in decades, who might be dead,
who *are* dead, or who live and remember pleasantly
how easily I was fooled? Oh yes I could. Do *you*
know how to stop? I don't think you do.

Last night coming home in the truck from the river
I sat in the back with the composer, who said the arts are about
being human, and so quick and hot I shut him up I said
no it's more primal, it's *biological*, they make
us human, we make our living human with them. Music enters the body
with the pure assurance of sleep without dream, or
life before memory when a child still makes himself up
moment to moment. That attention isn't *mental*, I said,
it isn't about *math*, or *subject matter*, it's
human life going on without stopping, I said.

You see, I know you've begun to play your saxophone again
after ten years. I know your sister's sending your son a flute
for his birthday. What will he know, that boy, when I see him
the next time, and the time after that?

Studio

"Drawing is the discipline most intimately concerned with touch."
—Jasper Johns

All afternoon she pulls paint across chalk and then rubs chalk on paint
      and then more of both.
The paint drips, she follows the long line down.
The chalk breaks to dust, and she goes to work with fingertips, heel of her hand,
      corners of a soft rag.
She wipes her hands on her jeans to change the tapes.
We don't talk.

I read all afternoon, while on my knees the baby squirms in and out of sleep.
I turn pages, pat and refold her egg-yellow blanket with my other hand.
When the baby wakes up hungry I hand her over to her mother.
I stretch, walk over to look out the north windows, where snow crumbles
      among dark pine branches.
It would melt at my touch, if I touched it, on the long walk back to the house.
I won't touch it, I'll hold the baby in her blanket, smudged a little
      with chalk dust, red, gold.

Solstice

The water gives up its hoarded chill
to the bright sun. The weather
pours us into summer

and we slide in the pool, splash each other
slide out, sit in a row
at the edge and talk until

the little girl says again, now
and again one of us shows her
she floats, her own body

holds her up in the water.
The big girl dives down
underwater and between

her mother's legs. You do it again
says the little girl to her mother
who obliges, with grandmother,

but that's not it, she'd rather
do it herself, and since
she can't yet swim underwater

she's mother, held up by
her mother while the big girl
goes under and explodes, daughter

of everyone, out of the bright water
into the bright air.
We could do this forever.

We can't leave, can't bear
to dry off, dress for the drive back
say we never will, never.

June 1995

Gifts

1.

Four wet inches
of unseasonable snow,
and my Vietnamese neighbors' children
toiled all Saturday to build a round fortress.
Neither parent helped. Their mother
came out on the porch often,
hugging herself, to give them
a general warning.

In Pennsylvania, when I
was small, my father built a snowhouse
as if he had researched the subject—
block on white block, and then
walled me in, only a window
for my face. I have a photograph,
but nothing to show
how seconds later I began to scream
in mindless terror. How I kicked
as he pulled me out, and the dome
fell in, and we left it.

Every minute, somewhere,
there is just such a misunderstanding,
as if we were all born with a gift
for giving the wrong things
to those we love:
the move to a larger apartment,
the house too close to the road.
A table set, a book
left open, a touch.

Time undoes most of this sad work.
But the child I was could not wait.

2.

The walls of the snow fort have melted now
To a broken circle on the green lawn, seracs
more grotesquely riddled and molded
than the rocks prized by Chinese architects.
Each is set firmly in a base
carved to fit no other shape.

Water Garden

1.

Decades ago we stopped by a shallow mountain stream
and you went upstream and down, while I sat by the leftovers of our meal
and tried to memorize the shapes water took, released, and took again
almost too quick for the eye— curving ribbons, gathers of white, glass
over the big rock, the eddy beside it— and the colors of the stream bed,
browns, blacks, granite and mossgreen, under a fitful reflection of pale sky.
I remember best the force of my concentration.

Years later we lay in sunlight on the sheared-flat top of a boulder
by a mountain lake, and I memorized the design of lilypads and tight buds
underwater and on the water, tracked the tranquil zigzag
of a duck and her mate. I tried to hold in mind a frame— the hatchwork
of dark Douglas fir against old snow. If we moved we'd disturb
the light covering of sun on our arms and backs, so we didn't move.
I wrote all this down and later lost it.

On another lake I saw only the shaken shadow of a mountain.

2.

We've never lived out a year in a temperate zone— one of those places
people set their tables in the garden for six or seven months,
places no one has central air. We've gone from one disaster area
to another, desert to swamp. Days on the plains, we'd turn home
from our walk to find black clouds had climbed the sky behind us—
we'd stagger home through thunder, avoiding trees, drenched and tender.
For months we've gone muffled and clumsy, waiting for the ice to melt
from our windows and cars. We've fallen asleep against the steady beat
of storm at sea, been waked by wind heading east or west,
shouldering our thin walls aside.

Now here we are again, where soft days are a tranced shift between
extremes: either pitiless rain flooding roads, orchards, every house in the canyon,
or the lockdown of summer sun.

3.

Today woodsmoke and fog drift in the air, trees and ground
are sopped black, and you are planning a water garden, to command—
like the Japanese courtyard, like the myth-bound medieval garden
that first enclosed the Rose— our composure. For months, I know,
you've been lugging home from trout streams higher in the Sierras
chunks of granite, basalt, and flamboyant pumice, one at a time
in the back seat, wrapped up in lichen and moss and blankets.
You went to the nursery and stared at what we can't afford,
and can— the names sent me to my notebook: the lilies Hermine and Candida,
and primula, calamus, rush, fern, every Iris. I suggest
we start the paced percussion of hollow bamboo on wood—
slowly filled with water to drop, to lift and fill and drop again
from its fulcrum, beside the water.

All this will take time and thought.
It will keep us occupied, as the groundwater of the heart
rises and falls in perpetual search of its level.

1997

Natural boundaries

Host

Autumn's fitful in the Sacramento Valley
stopping and starting like a schoolbus

Thin clouds blunt the sun
the high daytime moon fades among them

A blight spreads among the Sycamore
and Live Oaks, brown twists of leaf

but I've learned it's no real danger
to the life of trees, only another life form

a symbiote that makes its host
mimic the climb into winter

Everyone I've talked to for days
carries a story of slow damage

T cell counts, failures of chemo,
a mind emptying itself

and you, you saying to the love
of your life: no, no more

Loss happens so easily we can't
go back to see it begin or perhaps

it begins and stops and starts
and then we know how long

it has taken us to say "it's over"
and perhaps if forgotten moments count

so do the heart-stopped
moments when nothing hurt

Stars falling

1.

Alone in the room the child spins
the globe in its bronze frame.
Her finger touches here, where
she is, her thumb touches where they
are, the Japanese. She has seen
the real ocean. They are far,
far from here, yet again tonight
the black shades are pulled tight.

She puts a finger there,
across the other sea
where Father is.
She doesn't remember him.

2.

One week late in summer,
she is put to bed early
every night. The frantic voice
of the news speeds along.
She can't sleep until
the whispering women creep upstairs.

3.

In the neighbor's car they drive
downtown at night. Lights
dazzle on every corner and store.
She stares at the slither and blink of neon,
gazes and drowses.
No one's afraid anymore
of the other side of the world.

4.

Her window is left open. She can see
the night sky. Has she seen it before?
As she hangs over sleep, lights flare
against the black of her eyelids.
Father is coming home. She can't
see his face. Only all the lights
sliding like rain down the sky.

Whose arms lifted her from bed,
blanket-wrapped in the cold dark,
carried her to the porch
to see stars fall and fall? A man's voice.
The coal of his pipe glowing and fading.
She sits up in bed, she is weightless.
Her teeth chatter. Japan isn't far away.
The round world holds still.

Sun setting

1.

In the jeep, in 1949, my father and I
played how many miles to the next
bend in the road, ranch gate, highway's
disappearing point on a bleached ridge.

I always lost to the scientist. The dry air magnified
the bright land, I always guessed too low.

2.

We drove to White Sands
at sunset, where some men, after work
at the labs in the mountains
led us to the corner of a chain link fence.

Tumbleweed platted a hidden entrance
dug under the fence. My father lifted the tangle away,
sent me in first.

Something had happened to the ground.

My father said this glittering carpet
was trinitite. We walked,
slipped, listening to it crackle and shift.

Then we were there.

He hoisted me to a concrete stub
once liquid, solid now under my feet.
The western sky blazed.

Each man picked bits of the ground's green glaze
to carry away.

3.

For the next three summers, my father and I
drove hours north, miles from any road
on the Navajo reservation.
I'd stay with the jeep and my dog by a stand

of juniper or pinion, read my books
from the Gallup Public Library,
eat eight-ounce cans of Del Monte peaches
and Heinz baked beans, drink water
from the round canteen in its seeping canvas jacket.

I looked up often from my book:
Slowly , all day, the colors of rock and chaparral
faded, then deepened.
Peace rose and spread around me.
I knew myself safe in the wide world.
I was grateful to the old jeep,
to my father's job, that took us there.

4.

I didn't know what he mapped. He loved
to show things working,
was there a Geiger counter? Did I watch
yellow dirt dumped in a box
in the back of the jeep
where the trinitite had been?

What did I miss
reading Millay and Cather
in the late afternoon,
grateful to the sweet air?

Epeirogeny

>—n. (in Geol.) Movement of the earth's crust in
>the formation of continents and ocean basins.

1. *A circle*

At road's edge, the child squats to place one pebble
next to another. She has chosen them slowly, for size
and shape. Over days, she forms a circle
which she widens, moving them all each time she adds one.
One morning she finds them scattered. Half a dozen
left in place. She kicks these apart, and hunkers down
to begin the search again. She can count to ten. It occurs to her,
a simple invention, that each third or fourth stone can be larger.

2. *Igneous, metamorphic, sedimentary*

She learns these words from her father, and how to recognize
examples, too: marble, gneiss, granite, sandstone, basalt and clay.
In clay and sandstone her father reads fossils like characters
in a long story. Her fossil coral tells the age of the lost inland sea
where it bedded down. Her ammonite is younger— she loves
its dizzy design. Basalt pebbles line the high tide mark;
tiny crystals glint like stars in their dark, round skies.
She feels sorry for the long hard lives of rocks, but doesn't say so.
She gathers heavy words: matrix, telluric, fell field, rift, lithosphere.

3. *The world*

They move cautiously on the hill face. He flakes, with his pick and knife,
mica from mica until he can give her a sheet to see through.
On a cold day, they cross a lava flow. Only wind-scraped stubble,
scrub, and trees— stunted as if on tundra— grow in the drifts of sand
blown and silted among black stopped waves.
At the seashore, sand dollars, starfish, shells, take second place.
First they examine, with his old microscope,
the dozen names and colors of a handful of sand.
He measures her growth each half year
on the kitchen doorjamb; she stands a hundred times as scale
before outcrops, waiting for the picture to be taken.
They go down in a salt mine, a silver mine, into limestone caves.

4. *The garden*

On the plains, her husband built a wall of limestone,
quarried from the ground, pieced shape by shape,
without mortar, the old way. In California,
volcanic rocks climb up one corner of the water garden,
edge or sit sentinel to a turn of gravel path, a full plume
of grass, a small red maple. A drywall is begun
beside the redwood gates, the path beyond is flagged.
When they drive down from the northern mountains
he is always ready to pull over, should some cutbank or mound
hold promise. Late one summer afternoon, the valley all green or blue
before them— orchards, river, coastal range— they spiral slowly
down the road, arrive home with sunset, without a single rock.

5. *The world and the garden*

At home, in the brass bowl of the Russian samovar bought
one year in Athens, are stones picked up and carried back
from five continents. Agate, jasper and jade fill an enamel bowl
from China. These sets cannot be broken, though rocks can be added
if they are harvested with care, if they come late and sweet,
like this year's crop of stone fruits, almost ready.

6. *A new circle*

This necklace is of silver and coral, squash blossoms and beads between.
Little more than a century ago, the Diné began to work the silver
from the new mines. Though white and pink shell came over the mountains
or up from the south before the Spaniards, coral came late, in living memory.
This is pale branch coral, from the Pacific. She and her daughters
know the necklace has power, to wake and protect the sleeping future:

Raindrop, bead, yolk, rosehip, tadpole, swim safe in your inland sea.
Blossom, handful, keeper, we will rope you in, to this hard, shining world.

The Limits of Language

As I set out vegetables to peel, three voices
overlap each other: a refugee mother's,
her British interpreter's, and an American voice
making it simple. *Look at me when I am talking to you!*
In every language, mothers say that.

The voices build a refugee camp
here in my kitchen, pitching a tent by my refrigerator
as kidnappers sometimes set one up indoors
so hostages can't see out, see who their keepers are.

My first time in Athens— the onions and garlic done, I salt
the chunks of eggplant— all over town I saw motored tricycles
carrying charcoal briquettes, shoes, papers, sugar.
On their sides their name was painted: ΜΕΤΑΦΟΡ. Metaphor.
Carrying over. One place to another. That year the junta
was in power and artists in Athens went silent.
Watch out. Don't talk back. Be home by dark.
In every language, mothers say these things.

Most children in this camp, the mother is saying, don't have
mothers, fathers, anyone except each other. They feed each other,
she says. I put two tablespoons of oil into the pan.
My kitchen's a room where, say, Arafat and Netanyahu
try to work something out. Stalin and FDR. It's a no place.
It's the way the agents of our government preferred
to talk with Indians indoors, and through a "tame" interpreter.
Not in here! Not at the table! We negotiate in rooms
that no one loves, more no one's rooms each year.
I've kitchen-Greek. Melezani, rigani, maidano go in the pan.
Drink your milk. Eat your rice and beans, your taro, noodles, fish.

The marks of Bantu and Yoruba linger in Atlantic Creoles. Shivers
of leftover pain, of eyelids lifted on no meaning. So many cradle tongues
are lost now, we can't say them all— Sandawe, Warndarang,
Yahi, Nootka, those are some. I taught my children of languages and countries
on a globe useless today; the grandchildren have new ones.

Should we teach them this tent is pitched in the middle of each day, this camp
or target zone? Suppose we taught all the children to feed each other.
These people are our friends. Speak up.
Don't be the one to start a fight. Don't do as you are told.
You're not too young to understand.

1993

Seeing It

If you haven't seen it before,
you won't see it— not at first.
It is like acquiring a taste
for raw oysters or, better,
like what happened in the camps
the spring of 'forty-five. They ate,
but their stomachs had
forgotten milk, forgotten
jam, rejected it all.
                            Do you
remember the pictures? And
the pictures of the ones left
who didn't make it, to relearn
food?
            I was nine the summer
I found the bound volumes
of *Life* magazine. I told
no one, I went back again
and again.
                    A child's supposed
to have innocent eyes, but
I remember I put all I had of
experience, between me and that
final nakedness I was greedy for
again and again. Saw
white wood stacked for winter,
saw monkey faces.

Driving through sheep country
last spring, we said
to each other, "The willows
look like dancers, a slow formal
dance of willows," and we said
"Lambs can't be sheep,
they're another species
from these sodden masses
stodging in the grass, they
dance."

          The truck was about
a half-kilometer ahead
when we began to see
without seeing, we were talking,
but something in us registered
wood, pale sticks, yellow,
brownish, the whole truck
bed full to the top, a few
ropes where you would expect
a tailgate to be,
                              something
wondered why didn't the sticks
slide out?
          Then the heads,
the tiny hooves, and we saw
that most weren't even stiff,
were limp dead lambs, and
we laughed at our shock, we knew
in a second how this was a part
of the lambing
                    but I remembered
how at nine often you don't
know how things work, exactly where
your food comes from, or clothing
to cover you, or war.

The lambs that don't make it:
I learned the word for them, *slunks,*
but haven't learned the word— which is
not innocence— for not knowing
where it fits, where it can
possibly fit, what it is you see.

Three Poems

I. *Private life*

You know how, when you have been away from home long enough,
the rooms receive you grudgingly: a chair won't offer comfort,
counters, tables, seem piled with obtrusive objects,
light falls into emptiness you can't think how to fill.

Or how, when you have been a week trying to balance
the pain in your head, your fever rising, ringing, every day,
you wake up at last one morning and you're hungry
but you can't imagine anything you want to eat.

Or how, when you broke up your parents' household
you could find no place to put what you brought back—
the complete Kipling, the silver, the lidded jars
that once held the very meaning of *flour, sugar, tea.*

It's not enough to keep things in order, or keep them about
for decades, to dust or taste them lovingly, or even
to need them as we do. What is required is daily use,
the mind's map of that usefulness, territory

we must defend like any primate chattering at the borders
of need, making wild faces and gestures to ward off
strangers. Strangeness. We must be so faithful
to the boots in the hall, blue rug, white cup, beautiful map.

II. *City life*

Remember that night in Chicago when we missed an exit, locked
the doors, coasted through lights back to where we went wrong?
Or when in Kowloon or Marseilles or Houston we went down an alley
and were in another place: sleaze, or village, behind the gloss
of windows, marble, tourists, lawyers, armed guards?

Or remember back to when we moved or watched strangers move
into old houses, with plaster, brass *historic district* plates, paint,
polyurethane, matched tubs of natty shrubs? Or when we began to
look past people, as if in "custody of the eye," once the soul's
prophylaxis against all particular attentions or affections?

Or farther back, when we took our young distinctive skin,
ostentatious, across the lines and back, feeling safe— as people
used to say— as houses? Or rode the Metro until morning arrived,
imagining lives behind the ghastly faces around you, making them
up— you know now— because you've forgotten every face now,

because human memory for all its famous exponential linguistic
leap to tricks, shocks and lies, stops at our safe skins.
We lose people. And more. One day all the antique stores
vanish and we don't notice. The next day, all the signs to the
Autobahn, but we don't want to leave anyway anymore, what for?

What will happen next? Not car bombs, not a pandemic computer
virus, not our homely remodeled earthquakes, floods, hurricanes,
nor even wars. No. The burning city is history, the burnout
is between our synapses, brownout. Memory's next leap will
work a camera's slow pan back and back and out of focus.

III. *The News*

> *"Even if it was a fact it wouldn't be true."*
> —Adorno

So I work at it, like a character in an old-fashioned novel
who covers the walls with newspaper clippings, grouped,
juxtaposed, layered, obsessive. But real work, wanting
an answer, wanting an end. And no newspapers, magazines,
radio, television. Only first or at most second hand accounts—
stories, phone calls, letters, from *someone who was there.*

So when, in December of eighty-one, Zosia's letters stopped, I
waited. For eight months. Then letters from Warsaw came,
speaking only of her ordinary days— hours in line for bread,
holy water frozen in the font, Kuba's shoes. So I knew how
to write back. Later, there were couriers. Later, Chernobyl.
She wrote, "Nobody knows why we feel awful. Anyway we do."

So, in June of eighty-nine, what I knew about Tienanmen Square
I learned from my student Hong, whose father took a train
in to the provincial capital to phone her in Kansas, to ask

what was going on. The news was, there was no news. Or it was
our two hundred Chinese students marching with black banners.
Or it was the other students who did not stop as they passed.

In Washington our cab driver was Ibo; in Washington, an Edo.
Their news differed. Mariam and Amir could never go home to
Persia, but talked of their childhood during the long dinners
it took days to prepare. Not why they couldn't go home.
Sister Liberata, when she returned, asked us not to ask
about Nicaragua. Not just yet. "I need more prayer time."

And of course the domestic news has arrived daily, hourly.
I first learned of Cong ear collections from a student's
paper, in seventy-one. Now I hear he owns two newspapers.
When they nabbed the serial killer in our town, my friend Paul
who writes plays got an interview and found him too boring.
Nobody knows. Not just yet. Why we feel awful. As we do.

1990

History Lesson

"Where is the sleep that escapes such dreams?"
—Wendell Berry

When I arrived in St. Petersburg
after a night and day awake
it was the perfect hour,
October sunset golden on the Neva
on the splendid melancholy palaces.

Night closed quickly on the little apartment
where my son fed me and sent me to bed.
I slept for ten hours and woke from such
a dream:

Brilliant morning light
on the broad curve of the river, a fleet
of ships under full sail, blue, white, golden
and marching delicately up Nevsky Prospekt
a dozen elephants in draperies and tackle, white, gold, blue
and all the city's bells ringing changes.

This was not melancholy, whatever
it was. I woke smiling, hurrying to tell
my dream over tea and oatmeal.

You must have read about it, said my son.

No, what?

It's history, it happened. Those colors
are the imperial colors. That
was Peter's idea of how to celebrate
his new city on the marsh
on the margin of Europe.

I understood my dream then
though I had never before dreamed such
a dream about another
country. Outside my own country.

1994

Today

> *"Where have you disposed of their carcasses?"*
> —Whitman, "This Compost"

Who isn't transfixed by Mother's last day in intensive care,
or Jim, drunk when the car slammed off the midnight highway?
We come back and back, to handle, remember, fondle, imagine.
We keep our dead swollen with our tears.

And who isn't willing to march in the Plaza de Mayo with the grandmothers
of the *desaparacidos*, to send a thousand candles downriver for the vanished
of Hiroshima and Nagasaki, who isn't willing to hold the gas chambers
            and the chimneys
in the mind's chambers forever?

Whitman was right to be frightened by this earth and we know it.
We take in fiery destruction on each breath, our blood is a river
choked with the bodies of the other tribe, in our bones are the final,
            fatal beatings.

The dead are like children— they can't understand what we want,
and we can do anything to them, make them cry and cry.

Today I want to go on past the smoke, the weeping, the blank of impact,
past the day of death, past even what I know of days, years of systematic deaths,
I want to forget this taste we encourage in ourselves
as regular antidote to our awful indifference.

I want to loosen my hold, to be tender with the dead.

Remember with me Mother young in her evening gown,
the black one with the red flowers, the perfume of her goodnight kiss.

You know what to remember.

Imagine with care that afternoon near Zagreb, when Saba was nine,
and stood in her aunt's garden and tempted the butterfly to rest
upon her hand, and it did. Then all the family, eleven people, fell silent
to witness that.

Power

Rain mauls the skylight that seemed
a good idea in summer. All around, tall
Ponderosa pines, their tap roots deep,
not like orchard trees in the valley .
Not like the elm in Wisconsin which
one summer when I was a child
in a hurricane, fell through roof and beam
to lay wet leaves flat on my bare chest.

Power comes on in patches. Three candles,
enough to read by, six better. We talk of lines, transformers, towers.
A new way of dividing the night hours: now,
and six streets down, the Dark Ages. Somewhere, stars.

Connect the dots: all one afternoon Madeline sits
with crayons, making the animal cargo of the Ark whole and bright.

At the barbarous intersections, we all hesitate like learners.
Eye contact, feet nervous for the brakes. Sally showers
at her daughter's, Lisa does her laundry at Becky's.
In restaurants we complain to strangers at nearby tables,
swear, all of us, to put in gas stoves, gas water heaters.

Then we hurry to forget. Lots of hot showers,
a run on frozen food, meat, dairy, at every
lit up store, and motels do ordinary business again.
Two days and not one story, not one joke,
not one word to people we don't know.

The Quiet of Volcanoes

The year St. Helens blew, you could buy T shirts and book bags
with her picture, and the legend, *The Awesome Power of Nature.*
I used that book bag till it fell apart, as if it mattered
my childhood horizon was forever changed.

As a child, I played the game called Statues— we would all vie
to be stopped in the most difficult or hilarious pose,
not knowing life would do this for us anyway.

Volcanoes fling whole landscapes into frozen chaos. We
see beauty and order. When I drive north on Highway 97,
past Shasta, the whole central Cascade range is to my left
as I go. We think of these mountains as safe, imagine—
the sight of them consoles us. But even a sleeping volcano
can crack and collapse of its own weight.

We fear for friends who live innocently in the path of the storm,
the canyon fire. We fear for children, though there's nothing
we can do. Dickinson, who was often afraid, wrote that the lips
of the volcano never lie, put herself in the path of molten truth.

I remember our mothers used to send us out to play with the words
"go blow off some steam." Some steam changes the composition of rock.

Manzanita

"Within this tree/ another tree. . ."
                                        —Jane Hirschfield

This mountain town grew up
around the mines, so some of the trees
have nothing to do with me.
No one has fallen in love
with their rough or tender shapes
down at the big nursery, nor made money
from rows on rows of them.
Take the manzanita:
This small green tree dies a branch at a time.
After the first autumn storm,
her branches glow arterial red, and the one
that will drop off next year has leaves the quiet coral
of her small spring flowers. A few now already grayed,
incurled, thickened. Under the late sun
the pale leaves are translucent.
The long branch curves, reaching
for the floor of oak leaves, of pine needles.
It reaches and touches them.
Nothing to do with me.

Natural boundaries

"Our lives may rest on this; and our lives are our images."
—Muriel Rukeyser

1.

In winter, in Oregon, my father died.
When we drove back across the border,
I began at last to cry. Before his death,
I was certain of death, certain nothing
was beyond it, yet for a few moments I knew
how well he knew the state we left behind.
So that was how he left me, at the 42nd parallel,
which also marks borders of Nevada Idaho Utah.

Go outside. Learn. Pay attention like
the men and women who survived the Cascade landslides
in Oregon eight hundred years ago, and had
to move on, learn new salmon runs, new berries.
The Bonneville dam now drowns their story.

2.

Four years I've lived on two acres
of mortgaged California land.
Mort. Gage. From the Old French, *dead,*
and *pledge*, the Old Teutonic. The land
will be dead to me if I fail to keep
this promise. Would I rest easier
with a title free and clear?
The bones of Ishi were brought back
from Berkeley by ancestral neighbors
to be interred just south of here.

So I work at belonging until
the paths of knowledge are as thick
with information as a tree,
something that makes sense
to the senses and to the mind,
crowded with its failed promises
and its abstract fear of death.

3.

I know a woman raised in Berkeley needing
knowledge of her North California tribe,
small before disease and the gold mines
and the planting of grand orchards.
Grew up shy, feeling never just right
anywhere. In the Sacramento valley
she visits aunties and cousins. She asks them
for their stories, she is vigilant
and patient as the women who once
knew to the day which oaks
were ready to let go acorns for milling.

She watches, listens. It takes days to prepare
this bitter soup, this laughter, this precious bread
of acceptance. She comes north each year
at the same season, for the same harvest
of names, gaming signals, deadpan jokes, the sacred.

4.

I think of all the children born on lands
their families didn't know, taken
from there to boarding schools,
forbidden to speak in their own languages,
made to write letters home that no one
could read. Their white shirts, haircuts,
the way their fingers moved carefully, stiffly
over the paper. I think of an Israeli mother
taking a last look at her girl in clean clothes,
polished shoes, her hair tamed. The girl's face
in the last eagerness her mother would see.

On the third day of the trip they stopped at Naharayim,
an island in the river Jordan, known as the
"island of peace" since Israel returned it
to Jordan in 'ninety-four. You can see
Israel Jordan Syria all at once, from this
tourist attraction. "Forty eighth-graders filed out
from the bus to see the sweeping river view,"
the newspaper said. "Without warning. . ."

Perhaps you remember what happened
without warning. Remember, too,
how dozens of farmers out of Jordan
crammed the hospital halls to give blood
for the six girls who had been shot, keeping a promise.

Learn place, and learn each other.
Stay with the work. You may belong.
You may be safe, or one of those who saves.

Notes: *Ishi in Two Worlds: A Biography of the Last Wild Indian in North America*, Theodora Kroeber. Acorn meal is an acquired taste. The incident described in the last section was in newspapers for two days in the spring of 1997.

Rescue

After fire, wildflowers unseen
in thirty years. A few cars
made it up the dirt roads to see.

I used to wonder if I
could risk my life for another's.

I answered, thoughtlessly,
my small grandson standing
on the sidewalk looking up
Yes, that tree is dead

and gave myself
to the quick fire
that splits the dormant seed.

About the Poet

Sally Allen McNall's poems have appeared in such magazines as *Cincinnati Poetry Review, Cottonwood, New Letters, Prairie Schooner, Midwest Quarterly, Kansas Quarterly, Permafrost, Earth's Daughters, Room of One's Own,* and *Chariton Review.* She was a winner of the National Poetry Chapbook contest from State Street Press in 1997 for *How To Behave at the Zoo and Other Lessons.* She has read her poetry widely in the Midwest and on the West Coast. In 1982 she presented her solo script "Willa Cather" in the traveling Great Plains Chautauqua. She was also a Fulbright Scholar to New Zealand that year. She lives with her husband in Paradise, California, and teaches at California State University, Chico.